REAL WORK AT HOME OPPORTUNITIES

Kay Doliver and
Danielle Figueroa

authorHOUSE®

AuthorHouse™
1663 Liberty Drive
Bloomington, IN 47403
www.authorhouse.com
Phone: 1-800-839-8640

© 2012 by Kay Doliver and Danielle Figueroa. All rights reserved.

No part of this book may be reproduced, stored in a retrieval system, or transmitted by any means without the written permission of the author.

First published by AuthorHouse   01/04/2012

ISBN: 978-1-4685-3798-7 (sc)
ISBN: 978-1-4685-3799-4 (ebk)

Library of Congress Control Number: 2011963731

Printed in the United States of America

Any people depicted in stock imagery provided by Thinkstock are models, and such images are being used for illustrative purposes only.
Certain stock imagery © Thinkstock.

This book is printed on acid-free paper.

Because of the dynamic nature of the Internet, any web addresses or links contained in this book may have changed since publication and may no longer be valid. The views expressed in this work are solely those of the author and do not necessarily reflect the views of the publisher, and the publisher hereby disclaims any responsibility for them.

Although the authors have completed cursory research to ensure there are real opportunities offered at each of the links provided in this book, the authors are not endorsing any of them and have no personal knowledge of them, their creators/ owners, or their business practices. The authors have simply completed the basic research to compile the resources in one place and provided the information. You, the reader, should complete your due diligence to verify the validity and legitimacy of any opportunity you choose to pursue. Caution should always be exercised when providing personal information online to enroll or subscribe to any service.

Dedication

We dedicate this book to all of the unemployed Americans still trying to earn an income in this down economy; to the many American Armed Forces which protect our rights to be free to take advantage of these opportunities; and to the American economy which is always adapting. We know America will recover and be even better than before.

Contents

1. Introduction — 1
2. Mobile Notary Public — 5
   a. What is a Notary Public
   b. Links to the Secretary of State Websites for the 50 States
   c. Basic State Requirements to be a Notary Public in California
   d. Steps to obtain a notary public commission in California
   e. Marketing yourself as a Notary Public
   f. Notary Public Fees
3. Notary Signing Agent — 20
   a. Basic Requirements to be a Notary Signing Agent
   b. Steps to Become a Notary Signing Agent
   c. Marketing yourself as a Notary Signing Agent
4. Mobile Wedding Officiant — 24
   a. What is a Mobile Wedding Officiant?
   b. Basic Requirements to be a Wedding Officiant
   c. How do I get ordained?
   d. Types of Ceremonies
   e. Additional Services
   f. Marketing yourself as a Wedding Officiant
5. Site Inspection — 28
   a. What is a Site Inspection?
   b. Basic Requirements to be a Site inspector
   c. Types of Site Inspections that can be performed
   d. Marketing yourself as a Site Inspector
6. Secret Shoppers — 33
   a. What is a Secret Shopper?
   b. What are basic requirements for being a Secret Shopper?
   c. How do you become a Secret Shopper?
7. Research Studies and Focus Groups — 35
   a. What is a Research Study or Focus Group?
   b. What are the Basic Requirements for Research Studies and Focus Groups?

    c. How do you get involved with Research Studies and Focus Groups?
8. Clinical Trials   38
    a. What are Clinical Trials?
    b. What are the Basic Requirements for Clinical Trials?
    c. How do you get started in Clinical Trials?
9. Online Jury Panels   40
    a. What are on line Jury Panels?
    b. What is required to be on a Jury Panel?
    c. How do I get started with Jury Panels?
10. Virtual Call Center Agents   41
    a. What are Virtual Call Center Agents?
    b. What are the requirements to become a Virtual Call Center Agent?
    c. How do I get started as a Virtual Agent?
11. Virtual Office Assistants   43
    a. What are Virtual Office Assistants?
    b. What is required to be a Virtual Office Assistant?
    c. How do I get started as a Virtual Assistant?
12. Messenger Service   45
    a. What is a Messenger or Court Messenger?
    b. What is required to be a Messenger or Court Messenger?
    c. How do you get started as a Messenger?
13. Skip-tracer   47
14. Third Party Verification   48
    a. What is third party verification (TPV)?
    b. What is required to be a Third Party Verification Agent?
    c. How do you get started as a TPV Agent?
15. Close Captioning   50
    a. What is Close Captioning?
    b. What is required to be a Close Captionist?
    c. How do I get started in Close Captioning?
16. Transcription   52
    a. What is transcription?
    b. What is required to be a Transcriptionist?
    c. How do I get started as a transcriptionist?
17. Translators and Interpreters   54
    a. What is a translator?
    b. What are the requirements of being a translator?

    c. How do I get started as a Translator?
18. Writers/Editors   56
    a. What are Writers/Editors?
    b. What is required to be a Writer/Editor?
    c. How do I get started as a Writer/Editor?
19. Proofreading   58
    a. What is Proofreading?
    b. What is required to be a Proofreader?
    c. How do I get started as a Proofreader?
20. Artists   59
21. Cartoonists   60
22. Illustrators   61
23. Public Relations / Marketing   62
    a. What is Public Relations?
    b. What is required to be in Public Relations?
    c. How do I get started in Public Relations?
24. Online Education Industry Positions   63
    a. What types of positions do they have available online for Education Industry Professionals?
    b. What is required for these positions?
    c. How do I get started?
25. Subject Experts   65
    a. What is a Search Engine Evaluator or Internet Assessor?
    b. What is required to be a Search Engine Evaluator or Internet Assessor?
    c. How do I get started?
26. Psychics, Clairvoyants, Astrologers and Tarot Readers and more . . .   66
    a. What are Live Search Engine Guides?
    b. What is required to be a Live Search Engine Guide?
    c. How do I get started?
27. Search Engine Evaluation or Internet Assessor   67
28. Live Search Engine Guides   69
29. Posting Links and Ads   70
    a. What is "Posting Links and Ads"?
    b. What are the requirements to Post Links and Ads?
    c. How do you get started?
30. Blogging   72
    a. What is Blogging?

    b. How do I get started?
31. House Hunter or House Scout   73
    a. What is a House Hunter/Scout?
    b. What is required?
    c. How do I get started?
32. Craigslist, eBay, and Amazon Sales   74
    a. What is a Craigslist, eBay, and Amazon Sales?
    b. What are the requirements for posting ads?
    c. How do you get started?
    d. Things you REALLY need to know.
33. YouTube Affiliate   79
    a. What is a YouTube Affiliate?
    b. What is required to be a YouTube Affilliate?
    c. How do I get started?
34. Opportunities for Skilled Professionals   81
    a. CPA/Bookkeeping/Tax Preparers/Auditors
    b. Music Professionals (transcribers, arrangers, authors, and more)
    c. Nurses/Nurse Consultants/Case Managers/Physicians/radiologists, and some other medical professionals
    d. IT, Software Development, and other computer related positions
    e. Webpage designers
    f. Photographers/Videographers
    g. Travel Agents
    h. Sales /Sales Management
    i. Home Based Recruiter
    j. Insurance Industry Positions
    k. Packers, Loaders, and Movers
35. Never in a Million Years Would I Have Believed   88
    a. Get paid for hand written notes
    b. Get paid to drive your car
    c. Make Money with Mommy Branding Parties
    d. Publish your own Book
    e. Become an Astronaut
36. Places to Post your Resume for Work at Home Opportunities   91
37. Free Internet Advertising   92
38. Utilize Your Life Experience and Skills to Build Something   94

Introduction

The economic downturn took its toll on both authors as we ended up unemployed and trying to make ends meet just like so many others these days. Our solution, after a year of job searching with very little success, was to start our own businesses. It takes time for a new business to become profitable, though, so we decided to find other services to add to our offerings. Our research led us to finding a wealth of surprising opportunities to work from home using the Internet in many different fields of experience. The Internet has drastically changed the workplace and created many new opportunities that were not available just a few short years ago. Despite the number of opportunities out there, many people are still unaware of these new possibilities and still struggling due to lack of income. We decided to write this book as a way to share this information with the public in hopes that many will be able to start earning an income using this information. Please understand that we are not suggesting our readers buy or start a business or become an Internet Guru! Starting or buying a business can be complicated, expensive, time consuming and is not for everyone. Also, if you were an Internet Guru, you probably wouldn't need this book. As a matter of fact, the readers we hope to reach : (1) are trying to find a source of income, (2) don't have money to invest, (3) are looking for legitimate ways to earn an income doing what they have experience in, AND (4) would like to work online. Many of these opportunities will require you to work as an Independent Contractor or Self Employed Individual. This will mean that you will need to keep up with tax requirements as taxes are not deducted from your pay. Other opportunities will require employment. You will have to review each opportunity for all the pertinent details. It is important that you understand that these opportunities will not make you rich. Quite to the contrary, you will probably need to use several of these opportunities to reach your income goal. You will also need to market yourself to maximize your earning potential if you are to reach those goals.

We did not register for every opportunity listed within as we are not experienced in some of these fields, however, we did not want to leave out any important opportunities that someone out there could use. So, we did complete cursory research to ensure each link offered work at home opportunities without investment and we included some information on how to take advantage of each. A few of these links require memberships to participate that are nominal fees. However, other than a few work at home tools like a computer, Internet connection, fax, phone, email, and such, there should not be any investments or materials to buy in order to take advantage of these opportunities other than what is listed here. Each opportunity will of course require a skill set, in some cases licensing and insurance is needed, and they might have other individual requirements not listed within. You need to do your own research on each opportunity to ensure you understand the requirements and benefits of each. Remember the success of any business or work from home opportunity will be dependent on your ability to work independently, to complete projects on time and according to requirements, to communicate effectively with others, to handle your finances and expenses, and an aptitude for working with computers and the Internet. If you do not at least have those abilities, in addition to the separate set of skills listed, you should probably rethink your decision to work from home using the Internet. That is not to insult anyone, but working independently requires a lot of discipline and organization. You will be unsupervised and so must be able to still fulfill your obligations within the parameters of the job.

When reviewing the provided links, if you cannot find information on these opportunities, please review the careers page or Site Map, or you can contact the company for more information. Although almost all of the companies have open positions, a few are not hiring at this time. However, check back periodically because positions are posted when open.

Also, I want to point out that although there are REAL work at home jobs, some employment offers are not valid forms of employment and have the goal of getting victims to make an initial investment. We have tried to ensure that there are no such instances here, but it is only common sense to always do your own diligence to verify the validity and legitimacy of each and every opportunity you are considering. Never respond to check cashing, wire transfer or Western Union related offers. Never consider employment offers for forwarding packages and/or payments to or from foreign countries. And, I strongly recommend Anti-Spam/Anti-Virus Software to everyone who uses the Internet! Additionally, before proceeding, readers should review the Better Business Bureau Website and the F.B.I. Website, and other credible sources for information online scams. Being aware of the types of scams out there, and how they work, may protect you from being a victim of a scam.

We would have loved to find a way to share the information without a cost to our readers, however, researching, compiling, publishing, printing, and distributing this information required an investment of time, money and other resources. However, we hope the information is just as successful for you and worth the cost to you for the publication. We always welcome our readers input, reviews, comments, and/or new information on opportunities out there that we can share with others. If you would like to send us an email, please send it to realworkathomeopportunities@roadrunner.com and we thank you for your readership and continued support of our efforts to share information on work at home opportunity's with others.

If you are still reading, then you must be serious about working from home, believe you have the basic necessities for success, and be motivated and ready to go! So, let's get started!

Mobile Notary Public

What is a Notary Public?

A Notary Public is a public officer constituted by law to serve the public as a third party witness to the signing of legal documents. A notary's main functions are to administer oaths and affirmations on signed legal documents. This act is known as a notarization. Since the information provided on becoming a Notary Public below is state specific to California, you will need to check the Secretary of State requirements for your state which may differ. See below for the appropriate links for information on your state. Also, there are minimal costs required for this type of opportunity, but we have detailed basic information on what will be needed in the "Basic Requirements" section below.

Alabama	www.sos.state.al.us/AdminServices/NotaryPublic.aspx
Alaska	www.ltgov.state.ak.us/notary/index.php
Arizona	www.azsos.gov/business_services/notary/notaryqanda.htm
Arkansas	www.sos.arkansas.gov/BCS/Pages/notaryPublic.aspx
California	www.sos.ca.gov/business/notary/qualifications.htm
Colorado	www.sos.state.co.us/pubs/notary/notaryHome.html
Connecticut	www.ct.gov/sots/cwp/view.asp?a=3184&q=392266
Delaware	www.notary.delaware.gov/
Florida	www.notaries.dos.state.fl.us/
Georgia	www.sos.georgia.gov/administration/notary.htm
Hawaii	www.hawaii.gov/ag/notary
Idaho	www.sos.idaho.gov/notary/npindex.htm

Illinois	www.cyberdriveillinois.com/departments/index/divisions.html#notary
Indiana	www.myweb.in.gov/SOS/notaryapp/
Iowa	www.sos.state.ia.us/notaries/index.html
Kansas	www.kssos.org/business/business_notary.html
Kentucky	www.sos.ky.gov/adminservices/notaries/
Louisiana	www.sos.la.gov/tabid/70/Default.aspx
Maine	www.maine.gov/sos/cec/notary/notaries.html
Maryland	www.sos.state.md.us/Notary/Notary.aspx
Massachusetts	www.mass.gov/governor/administration/legal/notary/
Michigan	www.michigan.gov/sos/0,1607,7-127-1638_8736—,00.html
Minnesota	www.notary.sos.state.mn.us/
Mississippi	www.sos.state.ms.us/busserv/notaries/notaries.asp
Missouri	www.sos.mo.gov/business/commissions/pubs/notary/
Montana	www.sos.mt.gov/notary/Become_Notary.asp
Nebraska	www.sos.ne.gov/business/notary/index.html
Nevada	www.nvsos.gov/index.aspx?page=165
NewHampshire	www.sos.nh.gov/notary.html
New Jersey	www.nj.gov/treasury/revenue/dcr/programs/notary.shtml
New Mexico	www.sos.state.nm.us/Main/Operations/Notary-Open.htm
New York	www.dos.state.ny.us/licensing/notary/notary.html
North Carolina	www.secretary.state.nc.us/notary/
North Dakota	www.nd.gov/sos/notaryserv/
Ohio	www.sos.state.oh.us/SOS/Notary.aspx
Oklahoma	www.sos.ok.gov/notary/default.aspx
Oregon	www.filinginoregon.com/pages/notary/notary_commission/commission_app_renew.html
Pennsylvania	www.dos.state.pa.us/portal/server.pt/community/notaries/12609
Rhode Island	www.sos.ri.gov/business/notary/

South Carolina	www.scsos.com/Notaries
South Dakota	www.sdsos.gov/content/viewcontent.aspx?cat=adminservices&pg=/adminservices/notaries.shtm
Tennessee	www.tennessee.gov/sos/bus_svc/notary.htm
Texas	www.sos.state.tx.us/statdoc/notary-public.shtml
Utah	www.notary.utah.gov/notaryprocess.html
Vermont	www.vermont-archives.org/notary/
Virginia	www.commonwealth.virginia.gov/Notary/notary.cfm
Washington	www.dol.wa.gov/business/notary/nrequirements.html
West Virginia	www.sos.wv.gov/business-licensing/notaries/Pages/NotaryPublicCommissioner.aspx

Basic Requirements

To be a Notary Public, you will need reliable transportation, auto insurance, business cards, and a cell phone. You will also need to pay for training, an exam, an application fee, a bond, supplies and fingerprinting. This is all explained in detail below, including the sequence in which the steps need to be completed. Your investment will be approximately $300 for the training, exam, application fee, supplies, and fingerprinting. What is not included is the cost of insurance, bonds, and marketing which will depend on you. You can also comparison shop for the best price for these necessary items as there are many sources where you can obtain them. After becoming a Notary, you can list yourself and start making money immediately. You should consider additional training as a Loan Signing Agent to supplement your income.

Remember to save receipts for gasoline, paper, ink or any other expenses that are related to your income for use in filing your tax returns. You should also track your mileage if you will be performing mobile services as your vehicle expenses related to your work may also be claimed as a deduction. Consult your tax preparer to discuss possible deductions in detail.

Listed below are the basic requirements for the state of California taken form the California Secretary of State website at http://www.sos.ca.gov/business/notary/ to use as an example. You can click the links above for your particular state to get more information on your state.

Every person appointed as a notary public shall:

- be 18 years of age or older (there is no maximum age set by statute)
- be a legal California resident
- complete a course of study approved by the Secretary of State
- satisfactorily complete and pass a written examination prescribed by the Secretary of State
- clear a background check

Child Support

Applicants found to be non-compliant with child or family support orders will be issued temporary term notary public commissions. Notaries public found to be non-compliant after the notary public commission is issued may be subject to commission suspension or revocation. (Family Code section 17520.)

Convictions

State law requires all applicants be fingerprinted as part of a background check prior to being granted an appointment as a notary public. Information concerning the fingerprinting requirement will be mailed to applicants who pass the examination.

All applicants are required to disclose on their application any arrests for which trial is pending and all convictions. Convictions dismissed under Penal Code section 1203.4 or 1203.4a must be disclosed. If you have any questions concerning the disclosure of convictions or arrests, contact the Secretary of State prior to signing the application.

For specifics about your arrest(s) and or conviction(s), please contact the California Department of Justice at (916) 227-3849.

The Secretary of State will recommend denial of an application for the following reasons:

Failure to disclose any arrest or conviction;

Conviction of a felony; or

Conviction of a disqualifying misdemeanor where not more than 10 years have passed since the completion of probation. A list of the most common disqualifying convictions are listed on the Secretary of State website. When a recommendation is made to deny an application, the applicant has the right to appeal the recommendation through the administrative hearing process.

Steps to obtain a Notary Public commission in California:

Listed below are the basic steps required to obtain a notary commission in the state of California taken form the California Secretary of State website. Please review the following carefully as these details are completed consecutively and missing deadlines could be costly or extend the time for completion.

Complete Approved Education

All persons seeking appointment as a notary public must satisfactorily complete a Secretary of State approved six-hour course of study prior to appointment. (Government Code section 8201.) Please note that all persons being appointed, no matter how many notary public commission terms that person has held in the past, are required to take the six-hour course of study.

Current California notaries public with a valid notary public commission and who have completed an approved six-hour course of study at least once must satisfactorily complete an approved three-hour refresher course prior to reappointment. Important: An approved three-hour refresher course is only acceptable if the notary public applies for reappointment before expiration of the current notary public commission. If the notary public commission expires before course completion and a completed application is received, the person must take another approved six-hour course before being reappointed as a notary public.

The Secretary of State reviews for approval all courses of study submitted by notary public education vendors. (Government Code section 8201.2.) To locate vendors who have been authorized to provide an approved notary public education course; please refer to our list of approved vendors.

The goal of notary public education is to:

- provide proper training for all notaries public;
- provide a full understanding of the duties and responsibilities of a notary public;
- standardize knowledge for all notaries public; and
- reduce complaints and lawsuits due to negligence or misconduct by a notary public.

Upon satisfactory completion of an approved notary public course of study, a student will receive a Proof of Completion certificate. A Proof of Completion certificate evidencing completion of a six-hour education course is valid for a period of two years from the date of issuance. If a person seeking appointment does not pass the notary public examination before expiration of the Proof of Completion certificate, that person will have to satisfactorily complete another six-hour course.

A Proof of Completion certificate evidencing completion of a three-hour refresher course is also valid for two years from the date of issuance. However, a person seeking reappointment must apply and take the notary public examination before expiration of their Proof of Completion certificate and before expiration of their notary public commission.

Once you have obtained your Proof of Completion certificate for the approved notary public education course, you will need to do the following:

- Register for an exam by contacting Cooperative Personnel Services (CPS); and
- Take with you to the exam site your completed notary public application (pdf~64KB) form with the Proof of Completion certificate and a 2" x 2" color passport photo of yourself (stapled to your application).

Register for the Exam

All applicants seeking appointment as a notary public will be required to satisfactorily pass a written exam prior to appointment as a notary public.

Please refer to the following links for California Notary Public exam materials on the California Secretary of State website:

California Notary Public Handbook:
http://www.sos.ca.gov/business/notary/handbook.htm

California Notary Public Application:
http://www.sos.ca.gov/business/notary/forms/notary_app.pdf

California Testing Information:
http://notary.cps.ca.gov/

If you would like the above information mailed to you, email Cooperative Personnel Services (CPS) at NotaryInfo@cps.ca.gov OR contact CPS at (916) 263-3520.

To register for the exam, visit CPS at notary.cps.ca.gov/ OR call CPS at (916) 263-3520.

Take the Exam

Prior to taking the exam, it is recommended that the applicant review the Notary Public Handbook.

Allow plenty of travel time and bring the following items to the exam:

- A current photo identification (e.g. California Driver's License or Identification Card issued by the Department of Motor Vehicles);
- A complete current Notary Public Application (pdf ~64KB) form;
- A 2" x 2" color passport photo of yourself;
- The Proof of Completion certificate of your six-hour or three-hour approved education course;
- The registration confirmation letter; and
- The $40.00 exam and application processing fee (or $20.00 exam fee for applicants who previously took the exam and failed). Payment must be by check or money order made payable to the Secretary of State (cash is not accepted at the exam site).

Exam results will be available 15 business days after the examination. Cooperative Personnel Services (CPS) will mail the exam results to applicants. A score of at least 70% is required to pass the exam. Exam results will not be discussed over the telephone.

Successful applicants (those receiving a score of at least 70%) will have their applications transmitted to the Secretary of State for processing.

Each applicant not receiving a score of at least 70% will be sent their original application and re-take voucher with the fail notice. The examination may be re-taken, but may not be taken more than once in the same calendar month.

Checks returned by the financial institution upon which they were drawn are subject to a return fee and may be grounds for notary public application processing delay or notary public commission cancellation. (Government Code section 8204.1.)

Submit Fingerprints via Live Scan

Before submitting fingerprints via Live Scan, applicants must first take and pass the notary public exam. Applicants who fail the exam will not be required to have their fingerprints taken until passing the exam.

Prior to granting commissions as notaries public, applicants must complete a background check. To assist in determining the fitness of the applicants to hold the position of notary public, applicants are legally required to be fingerprinted. (Government Code section 8201.1.) Applicants must have their fingerprints taken within one year of the exam date. If fingerprints are not taken within one year of the exam date the applicant will be required to retest.

Applicants must submit one set of classifiable fingerprints, acceptable to the California Department of Justice (DOJ) for each notary public commission term. Fingerprints must be submitted electronically through the DOJ's Live Scan Program that takes and transmits fingerprints to the DOJ and the Federal Bureau of Investigation (FBI). The Request for Live Scan Service (pdf ~442KB) form is available online. Important: A notary public commission will not be issued until a report from the DOJ and the FBI is received stating that there is no criminal history. If the report identifies any criminal history, a notary public commission will not be issued until the criminal history is reviewed, evaluated, and found to be non-disqualifying.

For Live Scan locations and business hours see the DOJ's website at ag.ca.gov/fingerprints/publications/contact.php

You must bring the following to the Live Scan site:

- A completed Request For Live Scan Service form: http://www.sos.ca.gov/business/notary/forms/notary_livescan.pdf
- A current photo identification.
- A fingerprint processing fee and an additional rolling fee. Please call the Live Scan site to verify the amount of the rolling fee.

Be sure to request a copy of your Request for Live Scan Service form and keep your copy until you receive your notary public commission. It is not necessary to mail a copy to the Secretary of State; the information will be transmitted electronically by DOJ.

Await Commission Packet

The notary public commission packet will be mailed once the application has been approved and after the applicant has passed the background check.

The notary public commission packet includes:

- a cover letter with instructions;
- filing instructions;
- a notary public commission certificate;
- two Notary Public Oath and Certificate of Filing forms;
- a Certificate of Authorization to Manufacture Notary Public Seals; and
- A list of Authorized Manufacturers of Notary Public Seals.

Please be sure to review the cover letter and filing instructions thoroughly to ensure timely filing of the necessary documents with the county clerk's office. If you took the exam at least six weeks prior to the expiration date on your current notary public commission, your new notary public commission will not be sent to you more than 30 days before the expiration date.

Purchase Notary Public Materials

Once the notary public commission packet has been received, the next step would be to purchase the notary public supplies. Supplies required will include a Notary Public bond, journal, and seal.

Notary Public Bond

A notary public is required to purchase and file an official bond with the county clerk's office in the county where their principal place of business is located within 30 calendar days from the commencement date of the commission. (Government Code section 8213.)

A notary public may utilize any bonding or insurance company of their choice. Check the local telephone directory's yellow pages under the heading "Bonds". You can also do a search for notary public bond online. Be sure to get several quotes for comparison prior to purchasing the bond to ensure you get the best rate. You may want to also consider Errors & Omissions Insurance to protect yourself. Errors and Omissions Insurance coverage, also called E&O Insurance, is a specific type of business liability insurance that is purchased to protect against lawsuits resulting from an error or omission committed by the insured party during work that is performed for a client.

Notary Public Journal

A notary public is required to keep and maintain one active sequential journal for all their notarial acts. Journals may be purchased through local stationary supply stores. Be sure that your journal has sufficient space for you to record the required entries. (Government Code section 8206.)

Notary Public Seal

A list of Secretary of State authorized seal manufacturers will be mailed with the notary public commission packet. These are the only manufacturers that are authorized to make notary public seals. You will need to provide them the Certificate of Authorization to Manufacture Notary

Public Seals that you received in your commission packet.

File Notary Public Oath & Bond

A notary public must file an oath of office and bond with the county clerk's office in the California County where their principal place of business is located. This must be done within 30 calendar days from the commencement date of the commission. This 30 day period cannot be extended.

Statutes provide for filing the oath and bond by mail. It should be noted that the county processes documents in chronological order, but not necessarily on the date received due to the volume of documents. The oath and bond may be submitted to the county clerk prior to the commencement date of the commission and must be filed no later than 30 calendar days after the commencement date of the commission. You will need to take your Notary Public Oath and Certificate of Filing forms that you received with your commission packet. It is recommended that the oath and bond be submitted in person to guarantee timely filing. (Government Code section 8213(a).)

Dual State Notary Commission Information

If you are an Oregon notary, you may not become a California unless you are a California resident. Also, if you are an Arizona notary or Nevada notary residing in Arizona or Nevada, you would not be qualified to apply for a CA notary commission.

Marketing

Some online databases will charge an annual fee, but many do have free basic listings which can be used until your business is ready to upgrade. You should also obtain auto insurance, magnetic automobile signs and a cell phone. Some online notary databases can be found at:

www.notarypublic.com	www.notarypool.com
www.notary.net	www.notary-services.com
www.notaryfind.com	www.notary.com
www.123notary.com	www.notaryfinder123.com
www.findnotarypublic.com	www.gomobilenotary.com
www.notaryphonebook.com	www.gogetnotary.com
www.nationalnotary.org	www.mobilenotarysnetwork.net
www.notaryrotary.com	www.21stnotary.com
www.calnotaries.com	www.emobilenotary.com
www.thenotarylist.com	www.notarycafe.com
www.locateanotary.com	www.specializednotary.com

Other marketing opportunities can be found online by searching for law offices, estate planners and other professional services firms who may need a notary to handle legal documents for their clients in the field. Also, some states allow Notary Public's to perform wedding ceremonies, so please feel free to check the Wedding Officiant section if you are in a state where that is permitted to increase your service offerings.

Notary Public Fees

Listed below are the basic maximum notary fees allowable in the state of California taken form the California Secretary of State website.

> "A California mobile notary may charge any travel fee they feel is appropriate. Your fee should be based on mileage to

and from the locations where the notary is to occur. Please be sure to check your local Secretary of State website if you do not reside in California to verify the maximum fees allowable in your state."

California Maximum Notary Fees:

Acknowledgments	$10.00
Oath or Affirmation for a Jurat	$10.00
Certified Copy of Power of Attorney	$10.00
Proof of Execution	$10.00
Administering an Oath for a Witness	$5.00
Taking a Deposition	$20.00
Protest	$10.00
Serving notice of nonpayment of a promissory note or bill of exchange	$5.00
Recording a Protest	$5.00

Notary Signing Agent

What is a Notary Signing Agent?

A notary signing agent is a state commissioned notary public who verifies the identity of an individual by witnessing the signing of legal documents, and by viewing valid proof of identification of that individual. These documents are usually lengthy in size and generally require the expertise of someone who is trained in loan document signing procedures as well as knowledgeable of the notary public laws of his/her state. Signing agents are independent contractors who are assigned by lenders to handle the signing and notarizing of portions of mortgage documents. A signing agent can earn as much as $100 or more per notary service depending on the amount of experience they possess and their ability to present themselves professionally. Signing Agents must adhere to the notary laws of their state or jurisdiction. Signing agents are prohibited from giving legal advice or in any way explaining or interpreting the meaning of any terms or documents, and they are not permitted to prepare the documents, or alter them in any way. Becoming a notary signing agent can be a rewarding career move for those who possess the needed marketing and people skills.

Basic Requirements

To be a Notary Signing Agent, you will need reliable transportation, auto insurance, business cards, and a cell phone. In order to do the work of a loan signer and accept work from companies that are not local, you will need a computer and a laser printer. Some companies do still overnight documents to the loan signer or borrower, but most times they are emailed to the loan signer. You are required to download and print a copy to be signed and a copy for the borrower. Since there are often more than 100 pages in a set of documents, you need a reliable printer. A printer with dual trays is best as many documents are legal size. When the signing is finished, you will be directed to overnight the signed documents back to a specific address. You will be provided with a label or an address and the company's account number so you are not charged for the shipping.

Remember to save receipts for gasoline, paper, ink or any other expenses that are related to your income for use in filing your tax returns. You should also track your mileage if you will be performing mobile services as your vehicle expenses related to your work may also be claimed as a deduction. Consult your tax preparer to discuss possible deductions in detail.

Steps to Become a Notary Signing Agent

Some notary associations will provide Signing Agent courses. You will need to do your own research on this subject. As a Notary Signing Agent, you will need to complete the requirements in the Mobile Notary Public Section in addition to the following:

As with any business, you will only succeed initially through extensive training and continuing education. Therefore, the obvious recommendation is to attend courses and seminars. You want to make sure that you invest your time and money with a nationally recognized notary signing agent organization.

You will need to get your notary commission as some of the loan documents require notarization. Contact the Secretary of State in your home state to verify requirements. You can also contact the National Notary Association. They are a very reputable source for notaries, and can arrange for you to take your notary test in person or online. The organization can also inform you of the requirements and the supplies you need in your state. Notary commissions must be periodically renewed.

The NNA can also arrange for you to take a special course to be a Certified Signing Agent. In this course, you will learn everything you need to know about loan signing, including the function of various loan documents. It is a two-year certification that requires recertification at the end of the second year.

One important reason to use the NNA is that you will be listed on their signing agent website, which is respected and used by all the companies that need the services of a signing agent. The NNA publishes your profile, which shows your certification, where you are located and other details you want them to know.

Decide how far you want to travel to a signing and what hours you want to work. If you work directly for a lender, escrow company or title company you will be paid a higher fee. If you work through a signing agency, the agency gets a portion of the fee paid.

Marketing

Many mortgage companies require a substantial amount of experience before they will directly enlist you for your services. However, there is a multitude of smaller signing and title companies that will add you to their database and assign you work. The smaller firms typically have set fees and do not pay as much as the mortgage companies. Once you gain the needed experience you will be able to sign up directly with the mortgage companies who afford higher fees for their signings than do the smaller signing companies. As a start, it's a good idea to contact real estate brokers and mortgage companies. You can use other marketing strategies such as creating and distributing flyers, passing out business cards or building a website, and maybe go door to door to potential customers to introduce yourself. You should also join professional notary associations, and consider participating in online notary forums. Forum memberships are great for establishing relationships with other signing agents who can give you useful ideas for expanding your business. It will also help you to master the notary public laws, rules, and procedures.

Below is a list of links for signing companies and databases with which you can enroll to market your services.

www.specializednotary.com
www.MortgageConnectLP.com
www.UST-Global.com
www.ATSDocs.com
www.flsigning.com
www.akeenservice.com
www.bancserv.net
www.24-7nnn.com
www.americantitleinc.com
www.statewidedocuments.com
www.AnytimeServices.com
www.excelnotary.com
www.insuredclosings.com
www.nationalloanclosings.com
www.transstateclosers.com
www.emobilenotary.com
www.athomesignings.com
www.cpsignatureservice.com
www.docsigner.net
www.signing-services.com
www.cmdnotary.com
www.initialhere.com
www.docpros.net
www.signingagentnetwork.com

www.notarydirect.com
www.azmobiledocs.com
www.NotariesToYou.com
www.Docs2U.com
www.drititle.com
www.skyeclosings.com
www.americansigningservices.com
www.nnssinc2.com
www.notarysigningservice.com
www.tlsigning.com
www.executivesigningagents.com
www.udxnotary.com
www.centurydocs.com
www.xpnotaryclosings.com
www.americasbestclosers.com
www.flexclosings.com
www.essincaz.com
www.escrowquick.com
www.northernsettlement.com
www.docservusa.com
www.cdssigning.com
www.stratoslegal.com
www.dstitle.com

Mobile Wedding Officiant

What is a Mobile Wedding Officiant?

A Wedding Officiant is the person who performs a wedding ceremony and files the wedding license with your local County Recorder's office. They can also be referred to as a wedding minister, wedding clergy, wedding official, wedding officiate, ceremony officiant, humanist officiant, celebrant or justice of the peace. Choosing to become a wedding officiant can be an enjoyable way to perform a necessary service while earning an income. In some states, Notary Publics are able to perform Wedding Ceremonies, If this is the case in your state, you can also review the section on becoming a "Notary Public" for more information. You can also become a Wedding Officiant when you are recognized by an established religious organization. You should check the County Recorders Office for information on what is required to perform a wedding ceremony in your location. If only Clergy can perform wedding ceremonies in your area, don't give up yet. Modern technology has made it easier than ever to become an ordained minister. In less than 20 minutes, you can become a legally ordained online.

Check with local authorities, as there are restrictions in some states that must be met to perform weddings, funerals and baptisms—even though you are a legally ordained officiant or notary. Make sure that you read all the fine print when you are becoming ordained online as some sites are trying to sell things in the process of helping you become an ordained officiant. Read the information carefully to determine if the site is recognized in your state as a legal wedding resource. You should also check your county hall of records to ensure they have additional requirements you must comply with prior to conducting a wedding ceremony in your county.

Basic Requirements

To be a Mobile Wedding Officiant, you will need reliable transportation, auto insurance, business cards, and a cell phone. An email address and internet access is highly recommended.

Remember to save receipts for gasoline, paper, ink or any other expenses that are related to your income for use in filing your tax returns. You should also track your mileage if you will be performing mobile services as your vehicle expenses related to your work may also be claimed as a deduction. Consult your tax preparer to discuss possible deductions in detail.

How do I get ordained?

If only clergy can conduct ceremonies in your state, you can visit a search engine online and locate a website that allows individuals to become ordained online; some of the well-known ones are listed below. Select one and apply to be ordained as a wedding officiant if you so desire.

www.firstnationministry.com
www.ministerregistration.org
www.openordination.org
www.themonastery.org

www.ordination.com
www.wcm.org
www.ordainedministrys.com

Some ministries follow specific religious denominations and you will need to abide by their rules and ceremonies. There are however, many non-denominational ministries as well, where religion is not a pre-condition. Find a website that fits your desired denomination, if you have one. Many websites will welcome anyone who wants to become ordained through them regardless of denomination and will openly grant ordination without questions about religious beliefs.

On most sites, once you fill out the information, you are pretty much done. Many sites do the ordination for free, but others will charge. If you choose a site that charges, you will be prompted to pay before you complete the process. Some sites will try to sell you packages after you have completed the process. These items are not required, but you can purchase them if you desire. These might include certificates, minister IDs and reading materials. You can bypass all these items and still be a legal ordained officiant.

Once you've completed the required formalities, an ordination package is mailed to you, which may consist of the following documents: (a) Ordination Certificate; (b) Letter of Good Standing & Recommendation; (c) License card with credential listed; and (d) all information relating to wedding ceremonies and laws in the specified state depending on the website and package you choose.

Types of Ceremonies

There are a variety of wedding ceremonies that can be performed. The types include a Sand Ceremony, Rose Ceremony, Wine Ceremony, Unity Candle Ceremony, Lasso Ceremony or a Hand-fasting Ceremony, among others. You must also consider whether you will provide the prospective couple the ability to personalize or write their own vows.

Additional Services

When performing wedding ceremonies, you have opportunity to sell products as well. Some products that are easy and economical to acquire and sell to your prospective brides and grooms are the ceremony supplies. Unity candles, lassos, hand-fasting cords, wine glasses, roses and sand ceremony sets are easily found at local discount or dollar stores and the local craft stores as well as online. You can create templates for marriage certificates which can also be sold to your clients.

Some Wedding Officiants can choose to learn how to perform as a wedding planner. For wedding planning you will need to pursue avenues of education or study to learn what is needed to perform successfully and profitably. However, as a Wedding Officiant, you will be able to earn money working from home and make your own schedule almost immediately.

Marketing

You are now ready to market yourself. Below are a few websites where you can sign up to advertise yourself to perform weddings. Make sure you have studied your wedding ceremony basics and state laws prior to performing any ceremonies. You will need to conduct some research to learn what the going rates are in your area. You can also research the going rates online for the ceremony supplies.

www.weddingofficiants.org
www.weddingwire.com
www.weddingyellowpages.net
www.wedplan.net
www.gatheringguide.com
www.mywedding.com
www.bride1.com
www.theknot.com

www.weddingwire.com
www.californiaweddings.org
www.decidio.com
www.getmarried.com
www.weddingministers.com
www.weddingconnections.com
www.theweddingvendor.com
www.eventective.com

Site Inspection

What is a Site Inspection?

Field inspections generally consist of an on-site inspection of a premises and an interview with the designated contact. You will need to follow specific guidelines and requirements. Inspectors take photographs and complete a customized inspection report which is usually uploaded to the client's website upon completion of the inspection. There are a variety of inspections that can be performed without any licensing requirements or experience.

Basic Requirements

To conduct field Inspections, you will need reliable transportation, auto insurance, a digital camera, an internet connection, a printer, a cell phone, an eye for detail, the ability to follow instructions, and you must also be familiar with the internet as the reports and digital photos will more than likely be submitted online. When you accept a site inspection, the company will email or upload the forms required along with a list of photo requirements. Be sure to print the reports to take with you and review the requirements prior to each inspection.

Types of Site Inspections

Below is a list of some that can be completed with no construction or real estate knowledge or experience.

- Merchant Site Inspections

Merchant Site Inspections are needed when a business wants to be able to accept credit cards as a form of payment from customers, or provide consumer financing for its customers. Inspectors are required to verify the physical location of a business and validate appropriate and adequate inventory to conduct such business, while documenting important facts and information pertaining to the merchant's acceptance of credit cards.

- Drive-by Business Inspections

Drive-by Business Inspections are especially helpful to lenders who want to verify the physical location of an address or business when no personal contact or appointment is necessary. Inspectors are required to provide whatever documentation is requested (report, photos, etc.) to meet the needs of individual clients.

- Business Inspections

Business Inspections assist clients in determining the legitimacy of a business. Inspection of business facilities provide the client with the necessary proof that the business is who they claim to be. A physical inspection of the customer's location and that the information they have provided is verified for accuracy. Each inspection includes a detailed report and photos of the business. This inspection may also include proof of business ownership, appropriate business licensing, premises condition and neighborhood condition.

- Leased Equipment/Collateral Inspection

Collateral Inspections provide a way for our clients to learn about the physical condition, usage and/or whereabouts of collateral such as leased vehicles, RVs, boats and heavy duty commercial equipment. Serial numbers are usually verified and photos of the equipment are taken.

- Property Condition Inspections

Property Condition Inspections provide clients in necessary information on the condition and occupancy at any residential or commercial location.

- Occupancy Inspections

Occupancy Inspections are when inspectors verify if a home is occupied or not. It determines which entity or entities, if any, are currently occupying a property. Names, numbers, rental information, agent or/or property manager information and photos taken of the front of the home on each visit. Inspector may also be requested to make contact with the occupant or leave a letter.

- Vacancy Inspections

Vacancy Inspections are when you go to a vacant house and take a photo of the front and rear of property. You must verify whether or not the utilities are on and that the property is secure. If you can gain access, you will perform an interior inspection and take a photo of every room, boiler, hot water tank, any damages to the property and other items listed on the required report.

- Property Condition Reports

Property Condition Reports are detailed exterior and interior inspections. You will be required to take a photo of each side of the exterior, every room on the interior, the boiler, hot water tank, oil tank if in home, and any maid service issues, or any other issues that would deflate the homes value prior to auction or sale. Some maid service issues would include, but not be limited to: vacuuming of carpet, cleaning of sinks and toilets, dusting of counter tops and inside cabinets and draws, sweeping of floors and cob webs.

- Field Visit Inspections

Field Visit Inspections include components of other inspections, with added services such as customer visits, letter/document delivery and reference checks or verifications of information with neighbors.

- Collection Inspection

Collection Inspection is when a borrower falls behind or fails to make payments, Inspectors provide lenders the opportunity for a direct contact with the debtor. The inspector will visit the address, determine equipment condition and location, and personally deliver a letter requesting the borrower to contact the lender directly. In some cases, the inspector will be required to place the debtor on the phone with the lender.

- Vehicle Condition Inspections

Vehicle Condition Inspections provide a general condition assessment of nearly any vehicle type. The condition reports include verification of the make, model, year, vehicle identification number, odometer or hour meter readings, license information, and vehicle options.

- Bankruptcy Inspections

Bankruptcy Inspections are a visual, exterior inspection for occupancy verification. You will provide a property description. No interior access is required. There is also no requirement to contact the mortgagor, property occupant, or third parties.

Marketing

The list below includes companies with which you can sign up with to conduct inspections. There are numerous inspection companies online. Please do your due diligence in selecting the companies whom you want to work with. The companies usually have set fees for the inspections they request. However, you can feel them out to see if there is any room for negotiation prior to accepting the assignments.

www.quiktrak.com
www.photoinspection.com
www.metrositeinspections.com
www.nationalcreditors.com
www.southcoastinspections.com
www.usagapp.com
www.mmmortgage.com

www.secure.nvms.com
www.mcdarghconsulting.com
www.digitalfieldservices.com
www.siteinspections.com
www.advanis.ca
www.4smsi.com

Secret Shoppers

What is a Secret Shopper?

A secret shopper is a person who works as an undercover shopper who discreetly examines the way a company conducts business and the quality of their products and service. Then a report is completed on the shopping experience. This assists companies in making improvements to products and services.

What are basic requirements for being a Secret Shopper?

Secret shoppers should be able to follow directions, be detail-oriented, and have transportation to and from assignments as well as auto insurance. You should also have Internet access, an email address in order to sign up online and complete assignments, and sometimes a digital camera, scanner, and/or cell phone. Some companies will have additional requirements, so please make sure you check all details before signing up with any company.

How do you become a Secret Shopper?

To become a secret shopper, you need only register with companies who use secret shoppers. Selection will depend on when assignments are available in your area, but it will also depend on your personal information as shopping assignments are assigned to shoppers who would typically be a customer of the particular establishment. Below is a list of databases with which you can enroll to get started

www.caliberinteractions.com
www.mysteryinternetshopper.net
www.serviceexperiences.com
www.applymarketforce.com
www.thebrandtgroup.com
www.volition.com/mystery.html
www.satisfactionservicesinc.com
www.nationwidesg.com
www.customerperspectives.com
www.atopshop.com
www.a-closer-look.com
www.ardentservices.com
www.checkmarkinc.com
www.customerimpactinfo.com
www.focusonservice.com

www.iccds.com
www.intelli-shop.com
www.marketviewpoint.com
www.grassrootsmeasures.com
www.mystery-shoppers.com
www.qualityshopper.org
www.restaurant-cops.com
www.ritterassociates.com
www.serviceallianceinc.com
www.second-to-none.com
www.spgweb.com
www.serviceresearch.com
www.shopperjobs.com
www.hsbrands.com
www.spiesindisguise.com

Research Studies and Focus Groups

What are Research Studies and Focus Groups?

Companies conduct research studies to find out more about consumers tastes, preferences, choices and more. These studies give companies information which assists them in developing products and services. Participating in these studies is a great way to earn extra income while also providing feedback that can directly influence the decisions of top companies and have a positive impact on their future product offerings. These studies can be done online, in person, or by phone. Legitimate market research companies will pay you on average $50—$200 for about 30 minutes to 2 hours of your time just for giving your opinions. These business clients that are seeking your feedback range from small to large businesses. What they're doing is conducting marketing research studies to test their products and gain feedback about new products/services before they invest money in a mass marketing campaign.

Paid Focus groups usually consist of 8 to 10 people who join in a discussion led by a professional moderator. Often the participants in each group have common traits, experiences, or characteristics that allow the discussions to be interesting and informative. They will typically ask a few questions to qualify you as a participant. Upon completion of your focus group, you can expect immediate pay. There's a great amount of market research firms that are willing to pay you for your valued opinions. You will usually have to go to their office to participate.

Basic Requirements

To participate in research studies and focus groups, you will need an email address and/or phone number with which you can be contacted and reliable transportation. There are a wide range of different requirements. Once you register, your basic information will be used to select you for opportunities. When your information matches what is being sought, you are contacted. Sometimes, you will be screened via phone for more factors such as shopping habits, favorite restaurants, recent spending habits, or more before selection to ensure the right participants are chosen.

How do you get involved with Research Studies and Focus Groups?

In order to participate in research studies, you must simply register with the companies that perform them. You should review each website completely so you understand what is involved. Please remember that each opportunity will be different, and review the information on each site before signing up so you know all the details involved. These opportunities can be completed online, by phone, or in person depending on the company and opportunity. There are many other opportunities out there (some nationwide and some area specific) available. The ones in your area will sometimes have studies that are conducted in person and the in-person studies usually pay more. With a little Internet research, you should be able to locate a lot more opportunities now that you know what to look for. You can also search in the databases for shopping opportunities which you can request if you match the criteria sought.

For your protection, confidence and comfort, you are advised to do any additional research that you see fit prior to agreeing to participate in any potential paid focus group/ market research study. You should not have to commit to anything or spend any money to participate that is not reimbursed. Make sure you review every opportunity completely. Please also check the Better Business Bureau regarding any market research companies you choose to sign up with. The great thing is that you should never have to pay to get involved in any of these—so that eliminates the worry of losing money. If you want to find more relevant listings for your area, then you might try searching the Internet or your local phone book directory. I will warn you that this can become very tedious research. Also, be sure to watch out for all those bogus listings. Below is a list of companies with which you can sign up. Some of these sites are databases where you might be asked to pay minimal membership fees, and others will have no fees. Research each one and decide if each is for you.

www.inspiredopinions.com
www.findfocusgroups.com

www.plazaresearch.com
www.awr-oc.com
www.giveusyouropinions.com
www.focusgroups.com
www.advantageresearch.net
www.volition.com/focusgroups.html
www.athenamarketresearch.com
www.atkinsresearchinc.com

www.savitzpanel.com
http://losangeles.backpage.com/FocusGroups/

www.fieldwork.com
www.delve.com
www.fgglobal.com
www.focuspointeonline.com
www.2020panel.com
www.resolutionresearch.com
www.probemarket.com

Clinical Trials

What is a Clinical Trial?

Clinical trials are studies to develop an understanding of medical issues, pharmaceuticals, treatment and more. Clinical trials usually require medical testing and trial medication, but they also offer experimental treatment, compensation for time, transportation and effort, and a chance to make a positive difference in developing new treatments. Clinical trials may not be for everyone, but we have included the information for those who would be interested.

What are basic requirements for being in Clinical Trials?

Each trial is different, and the requirements/guidelines are different. You will have to complete questionnaires and some information is sensitive. However, these are clinical trials and in order to select the right participants, applicants must be screened for suitability. Some of the links provided are for databases which candidates can register with. These databases are used by companies that conduct these studies to find participants and they allow candidates more exposure which allows more opportunity for selection.

How to get started with Clinical Trials?

To get involved in clinical trials, you will need to submit your information. We have included links below to websites where you can register for these trials. Some links will be databases for participants, but this allows more exposure since these databases are used nationwide.

www.paidclinicaltrials.org
www.clinicaltrialsforyou.com
www.spauldingclinical.com
www.comprehensivecd.com
www.comprehensivecd.com

www.epharmasolutions.com
www.clinicalresearch.com
www.cc.nih.gov
www.clinicalconnection.com
www.clinicaltrials.gov

Online Jury Panels

What are on line Jury Panels?

As Attorneys prepare cases, they often seek feedback through mock jury panels on their cases. Online panelists listen to audio, watch videos, read material and answer questions and give opinions.

What is required to be on a Jury Panel?

Jury Panelists are selected through demographics, so there really aren't any requirements to list. You provide your information, and when you meet the criteria, they will contact you.

How do I get started?

Review the websites below. Once you have reviewed the opportunity, you supply your information by filling in a questionnaire and submit.

www.trialpractice.com   www.trialjuries.com   www.onlineverdict.com
www.signupdirect.com   www.jurytest.com   www.asksocal.com

Virtual Call Center Agents

What are Virtual Call Center Agents?

Many companies are now hiring for virtual office type positions for telephone work which involves customer service and data entry among other skills. You will work for companies that either utilize their services themselves or contract to provide telephone support services for others. Others might only require data entry assistance without telephone contact. You will have to review each website below to find details of the type of work offered or listed. Virtual call center agents (or home-based agents) handle in-bound and/or out-bound telephone calls or data entry work from their own home offices. Some positions will require some sort of testing or certification in order to qualify. These positions will hire people as Independent Contractors, Self-Employed Individuals, and/or Employees. Some even offer benefits other than income. You must complete your research to ensure your understand all the details of each.

What are the requirements to become a Virtual Call Center Agent?

Each company's specific requirements will differ; however, the following is a general list of requirements for a work-at-home position in customer service. According to most of these companies, a desktop computer is preferred, but a computer with at least the following specifications is usually necessary: A computer with at least a (a) 1Ghz processor (b) 512MB-1GB of RAM (c) a sound card and speakers (d) at least a 15" monitor (d) an up to date version of anti-virus and spyware protection software and a working firewall (e) software programs that may be required include Microsoft Office (Microsoft Word and Excel), WinZip and/or Adobe Acrobat reader

(f) a broadband Internet connection (DSL and cable are usually allowed but satellite, dial-up and wireless Internet connections are usually not. A wireless network inside the home is sometimes allowed) (g) a land line phone service (cell phone, VOIP, and cable phones are not usually acceptable and many companies require that this be a dedicated phone line separate from your home phone. Calling features on the phone line, such as call waiting, call blocking and voice mail, are often not allowed or must be disabled) (h) Web browser. Internet Explorer 6.0 or higher is usually required but a few companies prefer Mozilla Firefox, and (i) A Printer. Not all companies require printers.

How do I get started?

The following are a list of links to websites where you can register for actual work-from-home opportunities in customer service for some of the top companies in the country. Once you register, you will be in a database for companies to contact you as well as the opportunity to also search for and apply/register for opportunities as well.

www.alpineaccess.com
www.liveops.com
www.workingsol.com
www.arise.com
www.customloyal.com
www.acddirect.com
www.westathome.com
www.convergysworkathome.com
www.hirepoint.com
www.intrep.com
www.vipdesk.com
www.centurylink.com

www.advanis.ca
www.asurion.com
www.cloud10corp.com
www.ecallogy.com
www.micahtek.com
www.jetblue.com
www.newcorp.com
www.workingsolutions.com
www.service800inc.com
www.denihan.com

Virtual Office Assistants

What are Virtual Office Assistants?

Virtual assistants are people who perform office/administrative support from a home office. Having a virtual assistant, versus the typical in office alternative, saves the executive in employee-related taxes, insurance and/or benefits.

What is required to be a Virtual Office Assistant?

You will require experience in an office setting, an understanding of office procedures, equipment and functions, computer literacy, and a familiarity with certain types of typically used software at a minimum. Besides the usual requirements for these positions, you will need a computer and DSL Internet connection, a phone, a quiet work space at home, and the required software at a minimum. You will need to review the requirements of each of the opportunities below for any additional position specific requirements.

How do I get started?

Review the following websites for information on opportunities, their requirements, benefits, and other details. Each will explain the application process individual to the opportunity. Also take advantage of the additional databases for job seekers listed below to post your resume and search for positions.

www.capitaltyping.com
www.virtuallyyours925.com

www.assistantmatch.com
www.bluezebraappointmentsetting.com
www.teamdoubleclick.com
www.virtualassistantjobs.com

Messenger Service

What is a Messenger or Court Messenger?

When packages, documents, or other minor materials are needed to be delivered in other areas, but they need to be delivered right away, usually UPS, FEDEX, and the Post Office are not options. In these cases, messengers are contracted by phone, given information on pick-up and delivery, and any other information needed to complete the assignment. The messenger works independently as a contractor to complete these assignments.

What is required to be a Messenger or Court Messenger?

Typically, the minimum requirements include the following:

- (a) you must be professional,
- (b) self-motivated, detail-oriented,
- (c) able to follow explicit instructions, and
- (d) able to work independently;
- (e) you must have a clean DMV record,
- (f) a clean, economical, dependable vehicle that is in good operating condition and with valid registration and proof of insurance; and
- (g) You must be able to read a map and/or have a reliable GPS and know your area very well.

How do you get started?

You will need to register with national and local messenger services in order to start working as a messenger. A few links for websites of national messenger services are included below. After reviewing the websites, if you cannot figure out how to become a messenger for them, make sure you check the careers section or email their company for the information. They can send you information on how to apply with them. You can also do some Internet research to discover more national messenger services as well as more that are local to your area using some of the major search engines.

www.a1express.com
www.usacouriers.com
www.1800courier.com
www.nationwideasap.com
www.wcground.com
www.crossroadscourier.com

Skip-tracer

A Skip-tracer locates a person's whereabouts for any number of purposes. Many Skip-tracers work for debt collectors, bail bond enforcers (bounty hunting), private investigators, attorneys, police detectives and journalists, or by any person attempting to locate a subject whose contact information is not immediately known. This is a specialized field and you need to review each of the websites below for information on the companies, requirements, benefits, and any other details. Some of the links are for databases, but they are specialized databases where you can find positions in collections and skip-tracing.

www.webtracer.com
www.skiptracejobs.com
www.mycollectionjobs.com
www.ncogroup.com

Third Party Verification

What is third party verification?

Wikipedia defines Third Party Verification (TPV) as "a process of getting an independent party to confirm that the customer is actually requesting a change or ordering a new service or product. By putting the customer on the phone (usually via transfer or 3-way call) TPV provider asks a customer for his identity, that he is an authorized decision maker and to confirm his order." In some instances, this is required by law when selling goods and services over the phone and contracts are not readily available. Some companies that use Third Party verification are utility companies, telemarketing companies, long distance providers, cable companies, and more.

What is required to be a Third Party Verification Agent?

A Third Party Verification Agent should have experience in customer service, a computer with DSL Internet connection, a landline phone, and a quiet place to work at a minimum. You will need to research the requirements for each opportunity before registering to ensure you know what is involved.

How Do I start?

Review the links below and sign up with the companies which match your qualifications. The list below is just some companies that hire for this type work at home opportunity. More can be found online with a little research, but this should get you started.

www.bsgclearing.com
www.voicelog.com
www.electronicverificationsystems.com

www.directdtv.com
www.calibrus.com
www.realtimeresults.com

Close Captioning

What is Close Captioning?

Wikipedia defines close captioning as "the process of displaying text on a television, video screen or other visual display to provide additional or interpretive information to individuals who wish to access it. Companies are hiring for staff with good typing skills to work typing close captioning text." You have probably seen some of these companies on the captions while watching television.

What is required?

Of course you need to have good typing skills with few errors and a fast speed. Experience is preferred. Any other details on these positions can be seen at the following links. Besides the usual requirements for these positions, you will need a computer and DSL Internet connection, a phone, a quiet work space at home, and the required software at a minimum. You will need to review the requirements of each of the opportunities below for any additional position specific requirements.

How do I get started?

Check with the following websites on requirements, benefits, and other details. If you qualify, you can follow the directions for applicant submission.

www.ncicap.org   www.cpcweb.com
www.vitac.com   www.LNScaptioning.com

www.quickcaption.com
www.abercap.com
www.closedcaptioning.com
www.captionassociates.com
www.closedcaptioningjobs.org
www.vicaps.com

www.captionhouse.com
www.aicmediasolutions.com
www.captionadvantage.com
www.captionreporters.com
www.captioning.com
www.uscaptioning.com

Transcription

What is transcription?

Transcription is the translation of spoken word to written documents. Typists with special certifications are hired to type what has been recorded for legal, medical, financial, or other purposes of record.

What is required to be a Transcriptionist?

Usually experience and/or certification in transcription are needed. Other possible requirements include: a newer model computer with a DSL Internet connection, MS Word 2003 or newer, a typing speed of 65 wpm or better with few mistakes, a PC based audio player and pedal. In addition, you should be self-motivated, organized, and able to work independently. This list is not all inclusive, so make sure you review each of the opportunities listed before applying.

How do I get started?

If you have not completed the required courses to be certified, that would be the first step. You can find certification opportunities online. If you have already completed your certification, review the websites below. These are companies that either hire at home transcriptionists or they are databases where you can find transcription positions working from home.

www.cyberdictate.com
www.e-typist.com
www.emediamillworks.com
www.medifax.net
www.coniferhealth.com
www.eightcrossings.com

www.medigraphix.com
www.capitaltyping.com
www.appenbutlerhill.com
www.appliedmedicalservices.com

www.adeptwordmanagement.com
www.htsteno.com
www.tigerfish.com
www.medquist.com

Translators and Interpreters

What is a translator or interpreter?

A translator or interpreter translates from one language to another to effectively communicate between parties who speak two different languages both verbally and in written form.

What are the requirements of being a translator or interpreter?

Most of the following sites are looking for professional and experienced translators or interpreters who are native speakers of the language they will be translating. Some prefer a college education with at least 2 years of professional experience. Applicants should also be self-motivated, able to work independently, Internet savvy and possess MS Word proficiency. You should have a computer with a DSL Internet connection and be able to use any proprietary software. This list is not all inclusive, and you should review each website for specific requirements for each opportunity.

How do I get started?

Review the websites below for their individual requirements, details, and benefits before registering/applying. Each website will provide detail on application processes and requirements.

www.capitaltyping.com
www.lionbridge.com
www.csctranslation.com
www.elance.com

www.technovatetranslations.com
www.traduguide.com
www.translationcentral.com
www.translatorpub.com

www.outsourcingtranslation.com
www.avantpage.com
www.fxtrans.com
www.keylingo.com
www.proz.com
www.sdl.com
www.translatorbase.com
www.translatorscafe.com
www.transquotation.com
www.trustedtranslations.com
www.tomedes.com
www.worldlingo.com

Writers/Editors

What are Writers/Editors?

Writers/Editors provide and/or edit written material for companies online. They provide insight, direction, or information on content or questions from which the writer/editor has specialized knowledge, experience, or skills. There are 2 links below which will take you to sites that are looking for authors for children's books. You must check submission guidelines for each opportunity to verify if you meet qualifications.

What is required to be a Writer/Editor?

First, you must have excellent written communication skills, a command of the English language, grammar, and punctuation, a computer with a DSL Internet connection, a quiet place to work and knowledge to share. Since these opportunities are online, you will need to have a computer, a DSL computer connection, and the appropriate software.

How do I get started?

The following links are for companies who are hiring work at home writers or editors, or they are sites that provide listings for positions or allow you to upload your information for hiring. Make sure that you review the website for their requirements, benefits, and all other details so you understand the opportunity before registering. Every opportunity is different as the writing varies based on the type of website and its content and nature.

www.Patch.com

www.internetbrands.com
www.writersresearchgroup.com
www.suite101.com
www.allvoices.com
www.quarasan.com
www.cobblestonepub.com
www.contributor.yahoo.com
www.littletigerpress.com

www.families.com
(also forum moderator)
www.asbpe.org
www.copydesk.net
www.freelancevenue.com
www.demandstudios.com
www.dragonpencil.com
www.sylvandellpublishing.com

Proofreading

What is Proofreading?

Proofreaders generally will review text and make notes on any mistakes or corrections in spelling, grammar, or punctuation.

What is required to be a Proofreader?

Sometimes college and/or experience is wanted or preferred, and sometimes they are unnecessary. You will need to have excellent reading, spelling, and grammar skills. Besides the usual requirements for these positions, you will need a computer and DSL Internet connection, a phone, a quiet work space at home, and the required software at a minimum. You will need to review the requirements of each of the opportunities below for any additional position specific requirements.

How do I get started?

Review the following websites for information on opportunities, their requirements, benefits, and other details. Each will explain the application process individual to the opportunity.

www.proofreadnow.com
www.writingeditingservices.com
www.editfast.com
www.scribendi.com
www.wordsru.com
www.virtualvocations.com

Artists

The following link is for those with the skills of an artist. Artists can submit art works for greeting cards, books, magazines and more. Each opportunity has its own guidelines, so you will need to review the requirements and benefits of each of the opportunities below for any additional position specific requirements.

www.cardstore.com
www.psg-fpp.com
www.freedomgreetings.com
www.oatmealstudios.com

www.tradeleanintree.com
www.marianheath.com
www.papyrusonline.com
www.pkpress.com

Cartoonists

The following links are for those with the skills of a cartoonist. Cartoons and puzzles of all kinds are sought for comic strips, comic panels, and more for newsletters, newspapers, magazines, and such. Each opportunity has its own guidelines, so you will need to review the requirements and benefits of each of the opportunities below for any additional position specific requirements.

www.avatarpress.com
www.creators.com
www.darkhorse.com
www.funnytimes.com
www.imagecomics.com
www.kingfeatures.com
www.unitedfeatures.com

Illustrators

The following links are for those with the skills of an illustrator to assist with illustrations for children's books. Each opportunity has its own guidelines, so you will need to review the requirements and benefits of each of the opportunities below for any additional position specific requirements.

www.boydsmillspress.com
www.cobblestonepub.com-
www.dragonpencil.com

www.leeandlow.com
www.littletigerpress.com
www.sylvandellpublishing.com

Public Relations / Marketing

What is Public Relations?

Similar to being a Press Secretary, Public Relations is promoting a business, product, service, etc. to the public. Technological advances in recent years have made it possible for virtual public relations firms to flourish nationwide. This has opened a whole new opportunity for experienced communications and marketing professionals with flexibility to work at home.

What is required to be in Public Relations?

In order to be successful in PR you should have an outgoing personality, be comfortable with public speaking, and have excellent verbal, written, and interpersonal communication skills. Some specialized expertise and a college degree in journalism, PR, advertising, or communications is helpful. Pre-entry level experience and networking is highly preferred.

How do I get started?

The links below are for websites which hire work at home PR professionals, or provide a database with which to search for positions. Review what they have available. Please remember that each website will have their own opportunity and each is unique to that company, so check each opportunity for its individual requirements, benefits, and other important details before registering.

www.oDesk.com
www.Elance.com
www.schaafpc.com

www.Aquent.com
www.PerkettPR.com

Online Education Industry Positions

What positions do they have available?

Many students are trying the online education experience as opposed to the classroom. Public education has also opened up to internet possibilities, so the opportunities for employment with online educators is growing. This new trend is opening new opportunities for test makers, course creators and developers, tutors, teachers, coordinators, and other education industry professionals to work from home.

What is required?

Requirements will depend on the position and the company you are contracting with. Naturally, teachers will require the same types of credentials and experience to apply as with the typical classroom assignments. In addition, you will need at least a computer with DSL Internet access, telephone, email address, and be able to work within their online classroom environment. In addition, you will need to be coordinated, detail oriented, self-motivated, and able to work independently. You should always research the details of any opportunity before applying.

How do I get started?

Research the following links. Positions will be listed in the employment section of each website. Just like with any other job listing, the requirements and application process is individual and will be listed on each website.

www.brainhurricane.com
www.kaplan.edu
www.educate-online.com
www.teachforamerica.org
www.connectionsacademy.com
www.tutor.com
www.edufire.com

www.laureate.net
www.englishsolutions.ca
www.etutorworld.net
www.k12.com
www.aim4a.com
www.coursebridge.com

Subject Experts

The following links are for those with knowledge they would like to share and who would like to be a topic expert. The following websites give visitors and/or members the opportunity to ask questions in a variety of subjects from experts on those subjects. Experts supply answers via electronic means. Each opportunity has its own guidelines, so you will need to review the requirements and benefits of each of the opportunities below for any additional position specific requirements.

www.ether.com
www.ingenio.com
www.justanswer.com
www.webanswers.com
www.knowbrainers.com
www.studentquestions.com
www.hubpages.com
www.triond.com
www.suite101.com

Psychics, Clairvoyants, Astrologers and Tarot Readers and more . . .

Would you like to share your gift and earn an extra income? The following websites offer work at home opportunities to highly skilled Psychics, Clairvoyants, Astrologers and Tarot Readers who can give high quality readings while also giving the customer a great experience. If you think this is you, review the following websites for their opportunities. You can research for other companies online that offer similar opportunities as well.

www.keen.com
www.circleofstars.com
www.guidinglightpsychics.com
www.thepsychicsconnection.com
www.kasamba.com

Search Engine Evaluation or Internet Assessor

What is a Search Engine Evaluator?

There are companies out there hiring people who are able to do in-depth evaluation and research with search engines and provide feedback. Search Engine Evaluators provide feedback on search engine results by measuring the relevance and usefulness of web pages in correlation to predefined searches.

What is required to be a Search Engine Evaluator?

Search Engine Evaluators must be self-motivated, intelligent, Internet savvy, read and write fluent English, excellent web research and analytical ability, ability to work independently, a computer with DSL, and an email address. Some of the companies below also prefer people with a college education. There might be other individual requirements, so please make sure you review each website listed below prior to signing up.

How do I get started?

Review the links below and sign up with the companies which match your qualifications. The list below is just some companies that hire for this type work at home opportunity. More can be found online with a little research, but this should get you started.

www.butlerhill.com
www.leapforceathome.com
www.workforcelogic.com

www.lionbridge.com
www.clicknwork.com

Live Search Engine Guides

What are Live Search Engine Guides?

Live Search Engine Guides are a new trend meant to improve on the Internet experience by answering questions of members online in a wide array of topics. This is very similar to the Subject Experts except these are two search engines which provide the answers.

What is required to be a Live Search Engine Guide?

Live Search Engine Guides should be professional, enjoy learning and sharing information. They should also be internet savvy with a newer computer and DSL Internet connection. You should be able to navigate the Web, research topics, and provide answers. Most importantly, you must be able to work independently and reach goals. This list is not all inclusive, and you should review each website below for their individual requirements before registering.

How do I get started?

There are only two links below. Register with each after reviewing the websites for details. You can also do a little Internet research to locate more opportunities for Live Search Engine Guides. This is a new innovation which is sure to grow.

www.chacha.com   www.mahalo.com

Posting Links and Ads

What is "Posting Links and Ads"?

When you share a webpage or file, you're making money for someone. Websites and advertising companies make millions because of the traffic they receive from links online. Every time you post a link or ad, you can earn money. Residuals are not uncommon either. You will not get rich overnight. There are several factors which determine the rates you earn, and it takes time to learn to do this properly, understand the process, and grow the revenue stream. Given time, if you are motivated, and are ready to work for it, this can grow. Your efforts, and how quickly you learn, will be the determining factors in how successful this will be for you.

What are the requirements?

To post links you will need the ability to follow directions, a computer (you will want a fast processor and Anti-Virus/Spam Software), a DSL Internet connection, and some knowledge of how to operate a computer and the Internet. Each of the sites has fairly good instructions and information on how they operate, how posting links with them works, and how you make money. There will also be a list of answers to frequently asked questions.

How do you get started?

Visit the links below, and research each opportunity. Once you have researched the site, you should understand how each program works. The instructions are included and it is fairly simple to get started.

www.fanslave.net
www.linkbucks.com
www.linkvehicle.com

Blogging

What is Blogging?

A blog is short for "weblog". It is a website that has entries listed in reverse chronological order. It is similar to an online journal or diary that is updated frequently. The information entered will be based on your experience, education, and knowledge. Just posting information online in your area of expertise on blogs can earn you extra money. Many new software programs and blogging platforms have been created in the last decade to make the blogging process extremely easy.

How do I get started?

You type your entry, press submit, and it shows up on your blog. You don't have to be a brainiac to do this. You can even start your own blog as it is fairly easy, can be quickly set up, and can be completely free. Creating blogs could be good practice to prepare for this type of work if you have never done this before. Or, if you already know how to blog, just follow the links below and get started blogging for money.

www.linkvehicle.com
www.hubpages.com
www.payperpost.com
www.bloggingads.com
www.sponsoredreviews.com
www.linkworth.com
www.reviewme.com
www.shvoong.com
www.smorty.com
www.blogitive.com
www.blogsvertise.com
www.blogtoprofit.com
www.helium.com
www.loudlaunch.com
www.squidoo.com
www.wisebread.com

House Hunter or House Scout

What is a House Hunter/Scout?

Due to the state of the real estate market, investors have become very aggressive in their approach to locating properties. In order to find the best investments, investors are now looking for referrals to properties nationwide to locate homes that are already vacant but not yet listed for sale yet. This is done in your spare time by just driving around and locating properties, taking photos as required, and submitting the information to investors.

What is required?

You will need to be able to follow simple directions, have transportation and insurance, a computer, a digital camera and an Internet connection.

How do I get started?

Below are links to sites where you can register to be a house hunter. Once you are registered, you start house hunting. Each site will have its own criteria for properties which they would like located. You locate homes that meet their criteria, and submit the properties to them for payment. You can also research real estate advisors in your area to see if they do this as well.

www.keypropertieshousehunters.com
www.cityofangelshousehunters.com
www.libertyhousehunters.com

Craigslist, eBay, and Amazon Sales

What is a Craigslist, eBay, and Amazon Salesperson?

This section will be a little different as each topic has points I would like to single out. On this topic, this book should not be your only reference material. You might want to obtain more literature, or you can explore each site fully. Each site has detailed information for sellers covering every detail you will need to know. I will include the basics for each, and then you can click the links below to review more detail on each opportunity. Each is different in its own way, and all are great resources for selling items.

Wikipedia defines Craigslist as "centralized network of online communities, featuring free online classified advertisements—with sections devoted to jobs, housing, and personals, for sale, services, community, gigs, résumés, and discussion forums. Craig Newmark began the service in 1995 as an email distribution list of friends, featuring local events in the San Francisco Bay Area, before becoming a web-based service in 1996 and expanding into other classified categories. It started expanding to other U.S. cities in 2000, and currently covers 50 countries. On Craigslist most ads are free & can be "top-listed" every 48 hours and 15 minutes. The ads reach your entire local county plus some of the surrounding counties. Contact is discreet. You can manage posts more efficiently with a craigslist user account. The process of creating posts, editing, deleting, and re-posting ads that have expired is much easier." Placing ads on CL can be even easier if you learn to use the "My Account" features. Create an account, and you will be able to renew, revise and delete ads easier and faster, and you will be able to review all your ads on one screen.

E-bay is an auction-type website. Listings are listed for a number of days, sell to the highest bidder, or with the BUY IT NOW button at a fixed price. You can only list 5 ads for free each 30 days before being charged nominal fees after that. Selling fees include approximately 8% of your final selling price (these fees change periodically), and you have to calculate postage ahead of time. If your item sells, you then box it up, and take it to the post office. Contact is discreet, and the account can be linked to your accounts for automatic payment deposit.

Amazon provides an online marketplace for all kinds of products. You can easily upload product information by using titles, UPC numbers, and other information to search other like items and just choose to use the collected information to easily create your ad. The site uses customer ratings to rate sellers for buyer. You can easily use the web tools provided to create, organize, track, edit, and delete any of the products or information. You are notified via email when products sell, and after shipping, sellers upload shipping information online. All sellers must register for Marketplace Payments by Amazon. After you confirm a shipment they deposit the money into your Payments account every 14 days. Marketplace items list for free, but a 6 to 25 percent commission, a variable closing fee, and a $0.99 per-transaction fee are applied when a sale occurs. The $0.99 per-transaction fee is waived for Pro Merchants. You can review those options online. You can connect bank a account, and payments can be automatically deposited regularly per their schedule.

What are the requirements for posting ads for sale at these websites?

Obviously, you will need to be able to use a computer, be reliable or customers will not use you, you must have an Internet connection hopefully DSL, and you must be able to understand simple directions. You should be able to use a camera to take pictures of the items being sold, be able to do Internet research on products in order to create ads and price products, be organized and detail oriented as you will be managing many clients, products, items, and funds, and be able to put together great ads. You must have a phone and an email address as you will be the contact, and must be good with numbers because you will be handling money. You will also need a bank account in order to register on E-bay and Amazon.

How do you get started?

First, you will want to review each of the links below. Learn how each site works. Amazon and E-bay have sections dedicated to answering all of your questions on selling, buying, and more. All of the sites are organized in a way that is easy to maneuver around in, so you just need to explore. Once you have reviewed the information, and are sure you understand how each site works, then and only then should you began to practice. Sell your own items first until you get a little more comfortable. Then, if you like, you can find family and friends, and assist with the sale of their items for a commission. When you are ready you can post ads that you provide this service in order to gain clientele. You can also circulate flyers, place ads in other local media, use word of mouth, and other marketing options. Before you start to attract clients, you organize your business so you are ready to operate including deciding on a commission structure, creating whatever documents, spreadsheets, or accounts you need in order to keep your business organized and whatever other administrative preparation is necessary to operate this business. The steps to selling once you are ready include: (a) comparison shop for similar items in order to obtain information for pricing and for the ad (manufacturer's info, model #s, expiration dates, and all other details). You want to make sure you specify what is included and not included with the product for sale. You can also get more info about the item from the manufacturer's website. (b) collect photos of the item for sale. You can find pictures in online searches for your items. (c) put together your ad. You want to practice creating ads that will attract your desired customers and make them want to buy. (d) When potential buyers contact you, you will sell the items and (e) collect payment and distribute payment to clients. Your duties might also include shipping items depending on what your agreement is with your clients.

NOTE: Be honest with your buyers-if there are parts missing, damaged, etc., put it in the ad. Check your email and phone messages regularly and call your potential buyers back as soon as possible. Buyers can rate your service and you don't want bad ratings. When meeting potential buyers, please reme3mber for your own safety to follow some simple safety steps. It is best to meet at a neutral location, do not divulge too much information such as your schedule or your address, Do not accept cashier's checks, money orders, or personal checks, and if you must meet at your residence, do not allow them too much access to your home.

All of the links contain a list of things you are NOT allowed to sell/advertise? This list is not all inclusive. There might be more listed on each site than what is listed here.

- SPAM
- Anything that is unlawful, harmful, threatening, abusive, harassing, defamatory, libelous, invasive of another's privacy, or is harmful to minors in any way;
- Pornographic material
- The same item or service in more than one classified category or forum, or in more than one metropolitan area

Where can I sign up?

https://accounts.craigslist.org
http://pages.ebay.com/help/account.html
http://www.amazonservices.com/content/sell-on-amazon.htm?Id=AZFSSOA

A few other sites are listed below where you can list items for sale without cost for ads:

www.usfreeads.com
www.classifiedads.com
www.freeadlists.com
www.classifiedsforfree.com

YouTube Affiliate

What is a YouTube Affiliate?

YouTube was founded in early 2005 by three ex-PayPal employees. YouTube's vision is to give everyone a voice, to evolve video, and to make our partners and advertisers successful. Most of this section is straight from the YouTube Website in order to ensure their information is undiluted. According to YouTube, "The YouTube Partnership Program is a revenue-sharing program that allows creators and producers of original content to earn money from their popular videos on YouTube. You can earn revenue from relevant advertisements that run against your video using Google's proprietary technology. The program is based on cost-per-impression advertising. If your video content complies with the Terms of Use and Community Guidelines, and has thousands of views, it may be considered for the program. YouTube partners are content creators who have been invited to join our partnership program. They include established media companies like Sony Pictures and Universal Music Group; new media companies like Mondo Media, Machinima and Next New Networks; and YouTube web hit-makers, users who have created extremely popular videos on YouTube. YouTube partners are able to upload videos of any length and can monetize those videos by having ads served on them or by making them available to rent. In contrast, users are limited to uploading videos under 15 minutes in length and cannot generate revenue from those videos."

What is required to be a YouTube Affilliate?

The YouTube website states that, "There is no specific formula that will get you invited to become a partner. However, some general factors we consider include how often you upload videos, how big your audience is (e.g. the number of views and subscribers your videos have), the number of videos you upload, and whether your content abides by our community guidelines, including respecting copyright. Sometimes an individual video can become very popular. In these cases we will invite the user who uploaded the video to have ads accompany their video, and participate in revenue sharing. YouTube gives individual video partners the majority of the money generated from these ads. David After Dentist is a good example of an individual video partner. Once a user or company becomes a part of the YouTube Partner Program, they can monetize their videos by having ads served on them, or making them available to rent. YouTube gives them the majority of the money generated from these ads."

How do I get started?

Visit the link below and apply. YouTube states that to become a YouTube Partner, you must meet these minimum requirements:

- (a) You create original videos suitable for online streaming.
- (b) You own or have express permission to use and monetize all audio and video content that you upload—no exceptions.
- (c) You regularly upload videos that are viewed by thousands of YouTube users, or you publish popular or commercially successful videos in other ways (such as DVDs sold online).
- (d) Please note: all uploaded videos are subject to the YouTube Community Guidelines and Terms of Service.

http://www.youtube.com/creators/partner.html

Opportunities for Skilled Professionals

CPA/Bookkeeping/Tax Preparers/Auditors

If you are reading this section, you should have the experience, licensing, and knowledge of what the position is that you are interested in and what is required to perform the duties of the position. Besides the usual requirements for these positions, you will need a computer and DSL Internet connection, a phone, a quiet work space at home, and the required software at a minimum. You will need to review the requirements of each of the opportunities below for any additional position specific requirements.

www.humana.com
www.virtuallyyours925.com
www.tadaccounting.com
www.balanceyourbooks.com
www.bookminders.com
www.clickaccounts.com

www.vtaudit.com
www.batemanhouston.com
www.bidawiz.com
www.virtualaccountants.com
www.accountingdepartment.com

Music Professionals (transcribers, arrangers, authors, and more)

If you are a musician, play a musical instrument, write music or songs, and more, then the following links will lead you to opportunities in music. Since this is such a uniquely different category, all I can do is provide the websites below for your research. The links will lead you to websites where work at home opportunities are listed or to a database where you can perform searches for positions in your area of expertise.

www.cherrylaneprint.com

www.musicians-classifieds.com

www.eLance.com
www.musicianscontact.com
www.musicmates.com
www.booklivemusic.com
www.flexjobs.com/jobs/online-music

www.music-careers.com
www.gigfinder.com
www.taxi.com
www.mediawebsource.com
www.mymusicjob.com

Nurses/Nurse Consultants/Case Managers/Physicians/ radiologists, and some other medical professionals

If you are reading this section, you should have the experience, licensing, and knowledge of what the position is, and what is required to perform the duties of the position. Besides the usual requirements for these positions, you will need a computer and DSL Internet connection, a phone, a quiet work space at home, and the right software at a minimum. You will need to review the requirements of each of the opportunities below for any additional and position specific requirements.

www.cigna.com
www.sironahealth.com
www.workingsolutions.com
www.care-net.org
www.aetna.com
www.coniferhealth.com
www.fonemed.com

www.humana.com
www.consultadr.com
www.unitedhealthgroup.com
www.imagingoncall.com
www.thedoctors.com
www.resolutionresearch.com

IT, software development, web-testers and more computer related positions

There are lots of opportunities out there if you have the knowledge, experience, and skills to work with computers, software, IT, and more. These positions require different sets of skills and experience as they are many types of positions, so I will not list any more specific requirements. They range from software development to telephone technical support. Please review the details of each opportunity before applying. Besides the usual requirements for these positions, you will need a computer and DSL Internet connection, a phone, a quiet work space at home, and the right software at a minimum as you will be working from your own home office and will be expected to provide your work station. You might also need to be able to use new or proprietary software in order to perform the job functions from home.

www.askdrtech.com
www.supportspace.com
www.plumchoice.com
www.butlerhill.com
www.ockham.com
www.computerassistant.com

www.convergys.com
www.mysql.com
www.workingsol.com

www.icfi.com
www.artlogic.com
www.csc.com
www.advisetech.com
www.geeksontime.com
www.usertesting.com/BeTester/index.aspx
www.incontact.com
www.spectrumm.com
www.support.com

Webpage designers

If you are reading this section, you should be able to build websites and have the tools to do so from home. Besides the usual requirements for these positions, you will need a computer and DSL Internet connection, a phone, a quiet work space at home, and the right software at a minimum. Make sure you review the requirements of each of the opportunities below for any additional and position specific requirements. Please also review the IT section, and the databases listed towards the end of this book, for more Webpage Designer opportunities.

www.virtuallyyours925.com
www.internetlabor.com
www.schaafpc.com

Photographers/Videographers

If you are reading this section, you should have some photography or videography experience and you should have your own equipment and know how to use it to take and make great photos and videos. Some of these websites will even buy stock photos as they resell them. Besides the usual requirements, you will need a computer and DSL Internet connection. You will also need to be self-motivated, be able to work independently, and be detail oriented. You will need to review the requirements of each of the opportunities below for any additional and position specific requirements.

www.vfmleonardo.com
www.palmpressinc.com
www.tourthisplace.com
www.contributor.yahoo.com
www.demandstudios.com
www.BigStockPhoto.com
www.Photostockplus.com
www.CanStockPhoto.com
www.demandstudios.com

www.fastsnap.com
www.Shutterstock.com
www.ShutterPoint.com
www.Dreamstime.com
www.Crestock.com
www.obeo.com
www.Fotolia.com
www.iStockphoto.com

Travel Agents

If you are reading this section, you should have experience in the travel industry. You should be self-motivated, be able to work independently and meet deadlines, and should have excellent verbal, written, and interpersonal communication skills. It helps to be personable as this position can also be considered sales. Besides the usual requirements for these positions, you will need a computer and DSL internet connection, a phone, and a quiet work space at home. You will need to review the requirements of each of the opportunities below for any additional and position specific requirements.

www.workingsolutions.com
www.homebasedtravelagents.org

www.cruise.com
www.oasisagent.com

www.americanexpress.com
www.mickeyvacations.com

Sales /Sales Management

If you are reading this section, you should have sales experience and a successful past record in sales. You should also be organized, detail oriented, self-motivated, and able to work independently. Besides the usual requirements for these positions, you will need a computer and DSL Internet connection, a phone, and a quiet work space at home. You will need to review the requirements of each of the opportunities below for any additional and position specific requirements.

www.convergys.com
www.schaafpc.com
www.support.com

www.incontact.com
www.ncogroup.com

www.Patch.com
www,fonemed.com

Home Based Recruiter or Human Resource Professional

If you are reading this section, you should have experience in Recruiting and Human Resources. These topics can be a mine field to the inexperienced recruiter. You should also be organized, detail oriented, and self-motivated, be able to work independently, and have excellent verbal, written, and interpersonal communications skills, and be personable and outgoing. Besides the usual requirements for these positions, you will need a computer and DSL Internet connection, a phone, and a quiet work space at home. With a little Internet research, you should be able to locate more sources for similar opportunities now that you aware they are out there. The sites below are databases that will provide you an opportunity to search for Human Resources positions as well.

www.Infocision.com
www.virtualvocations.com
www.telesaur.com

www.internetlabor.com
www.flexjobs.com
www.hiremagic.com

Attorneys and Paralegals

If you are reading this section, you should have the experience and be licensed to practice as a Paralegal or Attorney. You should also be organized, detail oriented, and self-motivated, be able to work independently, and have excellent verbal, written, and interpersonal communications skills. Besides the usual requirements for these positions, you will need a computer and DSL Internet connection, a phone, and a quiet work space at home. You will need to review the requirements of each of the opportunities below for any additional and position specific requirements.

www.onlineparalegaljobs.org
www.lawcrossing.com
www.cardinal-ip.com

Medical Writers and Research Consultants

You will not be considered unless you have experience in Research and Medical Writing as these companies are looking for experienced veterans to provide content, reactions, thoughts, and answers in their online community. You should also be organized, detail oriented, and self-motivated, be able to work independently, and have excellent verbal, written, and interpersonal communications skills. Besides the usual requirements for these positions, you will need a computer and DSL Internet connection, a phone, and a quiet work space at home. You will need to review the requirements of each of the opportunities below for any additional and position specific requirements.

www.ppdi.com
www.covancecareers.com

Insurance industry positions

If you are reading this section, you should have the experience, licensing, and knowledge of what the position is that you are interested in, and what is required to perform the duties of the position. These links will be for companies that hire work at home insurance staff in a variety of positions ranging from underwriters and appraisers to nurse or case managers and insurance agents. Besides the usual requirements for these positions, you will need a computer and DSL Internet connection, a phone, a quiet work space at home, and the required software at a minimum. You will need to review the requirements of each of the opportunities below for any additional position specific requirements.

www.aetna.com
www.cigna.com
www.fara.com
www.careersathealthnet.com
www.humana.com

www.liveops.com
www.metlife.com
www.sedgwickcms.com
www.unitedhealthgroup.com
www.wellpoint.jobs.net

Packers, Loaders, Movers

If you are reading this, then you must be experienced in assisting people with packing, loading, and moving from one location to another. You can be a driver, a moving company, an experienced professional mover, or some other professional who does this type of work. Just review the website link below. Once you have reviewed the site, you can search for clients or list your information to be found. It is free to register on the site, but you will need to pay for a background check which is $41.00 which gives the visitors to this site peace of mind when contracting your services. Clients who are looking for labor can search for free but pay $1 to obtain a vendors contact information.

www.helpmemoveit.com

Never in a Million Years Would I Have Believed

Hand Written Notes

There is only one link for this category, and the category is self-explanatory. They want people who can hand write notes. You should have an excellent understanding of the English language, grammar, and spelling. You must have legible and neat handwriting, and be detail oriented, self-motivated, and able to work independently. Review the website for more information, details, and requirements.

www.ariacallsandcards.com

Get paid to drive your car

Get paid to drive your car, or drive someone else's for free. Advertisers will pay to wrap your car. No, I am not kidding. The following website is a database for prospective advertisers where you can search and find these opportunities, or list your information in order to be found by one of these advertisers.

www.thefreecar.com

Mommy Branding Parties

I thought this was ingenious. All of us, as mommy's, are always recommending things to one another. This company has created a niche, and made a way for us to earn money recommending things to each other. They have taken word of mouth to a whole new level by creating Brand Themed Mommy Parties where we can invite friends over, show them our favorite products, and earn commissions on sales. Review the website for more details.

www.mommyparties.com

Publish Your Own Book

If you are a skilled writer, and you want to publish your book, you should consider self-publishing. The benefits popularly listed for self-publishing are that you retain ownership of your work and you can get assistance from professionals in the publishing industry with experience for the production, advertising, and sale of your work.

If you have a work you want to publish, you can review the websites below for Self-Publishing Companies that will provide information on the process and requirements for this endeavor. As we have not personally worked with all of these companies, you should research each, review their offerings, and compare their services, requirements, benefits, and cost using the same comparative information to ensure you select the right company for your project. Review what each package offers, and make sure you ask questions. Review the Contract/Agreement to make sure you understand the legalese, and secure professional insight if needed to understand any documents before signing. Be sure to review production costs and royalties, understand what the markups are, and be sure you know how royalties are calculated. Each company is different, so make sure you review each thoroughly before proceeding.

If you choose to market your book yourself, you will need to create a Press Release and distribute it to major outlets. This is a little more complicated than it sounds, and professional assistance can only help. However, if you choose to do it yourself, information on designing, creating, and distributing your release can be found online with a little research. Also, you can research online to compile contacts for distribution to media contacts. I would suggest reviewing major television stations websites for station and affiliate information nationwide. You can also find information on major radio stations online. This might require some radio and television interviews to make people aware of your book. Make sure you are prepared for your interviews if you want to make a good impression.

www.createspace.com
www.authorhouse.com
www.xlibris.com
www.infinitypublishing.com
www.trafford.com
www.aventinepress.com
www.dorrancepublishing.com
www.publishamerica.com
www.magicvalleypub.com
www.llumina.com
www.dogearpublishing.net
www.wordclay.com
www.arborbooks.com

Astronauts

NASA is currently seeking applicants for the position of Astronauts in training. This position is so specific that I will just provide their link for your review. They are also seeking: Tram Drivers, Operations Personnel, and Education Instructors. Please remember that NASA's Space Center is in Houston, Texas, so you will need to relocate as these are not work from home. You can find more information at the following website.

www.spacecenter.org

Places to Post your Resume for Work at Home Opportunities

You can upload your resume and search for jobs in a wide variety of work at home positions on the following websites.

www.virtualvocations.com   www.internetlabor.com
www.telesaur.com   www.flexjobs.com

Once you register on these websites, you will be in a database for companies to contact you as well as the also having the ability to search for and apply/register for opportunities.

Free Internet Advertising

Additional marketing can be done by listing your services in local business directories online. Some major search engine directories, where you can advertise your services online with a basic listing for free, are listed below. When completing your profile, some of these sites will give you a chance to use search engine optimization for better results. You just select the appropriate categories for your services to ensure that you can be found in online searches. For instance, a Wedding Officiant would want to use Clergy, Justice of the Peace, Officiant, and Wedding Officiate to name a few. The Google AdWords Keyword Tool (https://www.adwords.google.com) can help you find the right keywords to promote your services. You also want to keep your profiles consistent so your company image can be maintained, and you should update these profiles periodically to ensure the information found online for your company is still accurate. You also want to ensure that you know what is being said about your services online. If you do not create your business profile, it will probably be appearing eventually online waiting to be claimed. You should claim these profiles, so you can build and maintain them, and prevent anyone else from doing so. Anyone can go online to comment on your business too. Many customers use this medium as an opportunity to praise or complain about your services. You, as a business owner, should always be aware what the Internet is saying about you and/or your business. It is a simple process to learn, and it can be very beneficial to attracting clientele. The basic profiles are free, but after you see results, you should consider upgrading your profiles on the sites that prove to be the most productive for you. Make sure you ask each new inquiry where they found your business, so you can track results. Another benefit will be that you can request recommendations from clientele to use on these profiles too. Consumers use the Internet to find service providers, but they also check online for what others have said about your service. If you don't provide good customer service, this can be a downfall and prevent you from attracting future business.

www.hotfrog.com
www.bingbusinessportal.com
www.yellowbot.com
www.expressupdateusa.com
www.supermedia.com
www.yellowbook360.com
www.advertise.local.com
www.biz.yelp.com
www.business.angieslist.com
www.listings.mapquest.com
www.listings.local.yahoo.com
www.google.com
www.inter800.com
www.cityslick.net
www.geolocal.com
www.metrobot.com
www.merchantcircle.com

Utilize Your Life Experience and Skills to Build Something

Each of us has acquired different types of experience and skills sets throughout our lives that make our strengths unique. Think about what you have learned that makes you unique and provides a valuable service in the marketplace. We can all use our experience as independent contractors to build our own client base. It may be a scary concept not to have the employer to fall back on. However, for those who need an income, it may be the solution. We are going to list an example to get you in the right mindset so you can figure it out on your own.

If you have a Green Thumb and enjoy gardening, starting a landscaping business would be a great way to earn an extra income. Those gardening skills are the key component, but you should also be able to talk to customers; be able to do simple math calculations to prepare accurate bids; be able to handle the administrative tasks like bookkeeping, banking, reporting, scheduling, and such or have someone else assist because these details ARE important; and be able to complete the tasks you are contracted to complete. Word of Mouth follows good workmanship and customer service, and this is the BEST form of advertising. You must bear in mind that landscaping is hard work; require long periods outdoors, sometimes in unpleasant weather. You should also research city and county licensing requirements, and make sure you keep up with insurance and tax requirements too. Some requirements for this industry include that service is allowed only for maintenance and repairs under a certain dollar amount (no installation) without a contractor's license. Contractor Licenses are State specific and can be found online for your state. City licenses are required for cities where you perform work. Liability Insurance is a must, but you can shop around. Sometimes it is possible to use your personal insurance agent and get a multi-discount. This is important protection and can cost much less than you think. Of course, you will also need the tools of the trade which include a cell phone with a decent rate plan, business cards, car magnets, a truck, lawnmower, shovels, weed eater and such. If you need to rent equipment, you can find equipment rental companies in search engines and the good old fashioned yellow pages. It also helps to create accounts with the supply stores you frequent because you can earn rewards and discounts. Wholesalers of landscaping supplies, equipment, materials and plants will provide better pricing than the retailers. However, to set up a wholesale account, you will need your business license. The simplest way to market yourself is to drive around and distribute flyers to properties that obviously need your services. Some properties may be undeveloped land with no building or tenant. If there are signs for property management companies, development companies, real estate companies, or other, you can contact those numbers to see if they will either pass along your information or give you forwarding information. If a property is managed off site, sometimes they appreciate someone letting them know when service is really needed and may contract you. If there are no signs, you can search property information on your county assessor's website. This will provide you with hopefully a name and address, so you can mail your flyer to the right person. If you prefer to work from home to market, you can search property management and real estate companies online and contact them to become a vendor for landscaping properties they manage in your area. You should also review the Advertising Section to find out how you can list your services in many of the major online search engines and receive calls from potential customers who are searching for your services online!

Keep in mind that when selecting your chosen service, it must cater to your strengths, skills and abilities. You must consider the benefits you are looking for in your opportunity. For instance, if you have a bad back, you do not like to get dirty or you are not mechanically inclined, a landscaping business would obviously be a bad decision. You are obviously going to get dirty, equipment frequently breaks down and will need onsite repairs and much of the equipment can be heavy and will require strength and endurance to push or carry. If you select gardening, you would also have to consider protective equipment to prevent injuries.

Hopefully this section has you thinking about how your skills, strengths and experience will fit in the marketplace.

In closing, we hope this book helps others to achieve their goal of working at home. Good Luck!

www.ingramcontent.com/pod-product-compliance
Lightning Source LLC
Chambersburg PA
CBHW030858180526
45163CB00004B/1627